The *best* part
of being a leader?

Dealing with people!

The *worst* part
of being a leader?

Same answer!

POSITIVE DISCIPLINE®

How To Resolve Tough Performance Problems Quickly ... and Permanently

Eric Harvey   Paul Sims

Resources for Personal and Professional Success

POSITIVE DISCIPLINE®

Printed in the United States of America.

20 19 18 17 16 15 14 13 12

Edited by Michelle Sedas
Produced and designed by Steve Ventura
Printed by Cedar Graphics

ISBN 1-885228-62-7

9 781885 228628   90000

INTRODUCTION

If you're like most leaders, you've undoubtedly spent some time in that frustrating zone *between a rock and a hard place*. On one hand, you're responsible for accomplishing the goals and objectives of the organization … for making sure the job gets done. On the other hand, you have to get that job done with and through other people. And those people have agendas of their own – agendas that sometimes run counter to the goals of the business and your personal expectations. Two conflicting realities, one you … right in the middle. **Ouch!**

To be sure, there are definite benefits (and accompanying perks) to being a leader. You're in charge … you get to call the shots. But headaches come with the territory as well.

No one has to tell you that leadership is challenging. The demands on you (and your time) are increasing – as are the number and complexity of obstacles you must face. And typically, the most intense and gut-wrenching of these obstacles fall in the category labeled with those three dreaded words:

employee performance problems.

The good news is that the vast majority of employees want to do well and try hard to do so. Most people are on target most of the time. They come in, do their jobs, and then go home – causing you few, if any, problems.

The bad news: nobody's perfect. Everyone occasionally makes a mistake that needs to be addressed (by you), and corrected and avoided (by him or her) in the future.

The worse news: there are a few people out there who are just plain difficult; they aren't good team members … they can't or won't perform as expected. Though small in number, this group can cause a lot of disruption within your workplace – not to mention a bunch of sleepless nights for "you know who"! And, of course, despite any emotion you may be experiencing, you're expected to calmly and professionally deal with these problems in ways that are in sync with: a) the values and procedures of your organization; b) all applicable laws and governmental regulations; and c) reasonable expectations of fair and consistent treatment.

Welcome to more of that land between a rock and a hard place!

The Avoidance Trap

Few leaders wake up thinking, "Oh good, I get to go in and chew somebody out today!" How about you?

When you face the prospect of confronting someone about a performance problem, do you dread it … worry about it … get stressed-out? If your answer is yes, you're not alone! Most managers agree that "taking disciplinary action" is the absolute worst part of their jobs. Many hate it so much that they look for every excuse to avoid it altogether. And they justify their inaction with all-too-common rationalizations like …

The employee's performance really isn't THAT bad.

> WRONG! If it's negatively affecting people or results (which it probably is) – if it's bothering you and causing you some level of discomfort (which it *obviously* is) – then it's "bad" enough to require corrective action.

Eventually, the problem will go away on its own.

> WRONG! If the problem isn't addressed and corrected, chances are greater that it will continue … or get even worse.

I'm too busy. I don't have the time to deal with it.

> WRONG! Even if you're busy (as most leaders are), you have to *make* the time. Like the old saying goes: You can pay now, or you can pay later … with interest!

It's not MY problem. My boss, HR, or someone else should handle it.

> WRONG! That's looking for a scapegoat and shirking leadership responsibility. Addressing performance problems of the people you lead is a critical part of your job.

I'm not sure what to do … I don't know how.

> COULD BE!

Only one of these rationalizations (excuses) has real validity: *I don't know how.* A leader's lack of problem-solving skills and techniques can cause discomfort, diminish confidence, and ultimately lead to poor results. It's just plain hard to do a good job when you don't have the right "tools."

Fact is, far too many leaders are ill prepared to effectively address employee performance problems … and it shows. It takes its toll – on their organizations *and* the leaders themselves. But it doesn't have to be that way.

That's why we wrote this book. That's why you'll want to pay attention to what you're about to read. Through the information that follows, you'll learn how to use POSITIVE DISCIPLINE® – a practical, time-tested approach to resolving performance problems … and strengthening employee commitment in the process.

Whether you're an executive, manager, supervisor, or team leader – whether you're new to the job or have been in leadership for some time – POSITIVE DISCIPLINE will help you better navigate in that land between a rock and a hard place. You'll discover how to minimize the intense emotions that typically accompany performance discrepancies. And you'll uncover the secrets to getting the **results** you want and need – ones that are based on a new, more accurate, and more *positive* understanding of what "discipline" is really about. As a result, you'll be a better, more confident leader … for your organization, for your team, and for yourself.

In the real world, there are no guarantees that you'll always be successful at addressing workplace issues. But, if you practice the strategies and methods that follow, you'll be successful *most* of the time. You won't need to fear (or avoid) taking corrective action.

You will know how!

CONTENTS

Little value
comes out of the
common belief that
discipline and
punishment
go hand in hand.

REDEFINING "DISCIPLINE"

When you hear the word "discipline," do you think of punishment … pain … something you do to others for misbehavior? Most people do. Let's face it – there's a lot of negative baggage associated with that term! And it probably started back in childhood.

Do you remember being on the receiving end of some form of "discipline" doled out by a relative, a teacher, a school principal, an athletic coach, or some other person who had authority over you? Were your ever "grounded"? Ever "benched"? Maybe even "suspended"? It hurt! It was humiliating! Truth be told, it wasn't pleasant for those parents, teachers, or coaches either. And while nobody liked it, it was (and still is) a common *modus operandi*.

The Traditional Approach

According to traditional ("old school") thinking, punishment is the most direct way to deal with performance problems. The *theory* is quite simple: If you inflict enough pain on those who misbehave, you'll eventually get their attention and they'll start doing what you want them to. And the *message* is clear: "Since you screwed up, I'm going to do something bad to you. And if you don't get better, you're gonna get something even worse!"

While both the theory and message may work in some life situations, they tend to backfire when applied to adults on the job. Why? Because they're based upon the **fallacy** that people will respond progressively better when treated progressively worse. Think about that for a moment. It's just not realistic! Fact is, punishment typically produces feelings of rejection, frustration, and humiliation. Rather than motivating employees to become better performers, it's more likely to teach them that they should merely avoid getting caught! Some "retire on the job" and do as little as they can get away with. Worse yet, others decide to "get even" and do things intended to cause problems for you, your team, and your entire organization.

So, punishing employees can actually make things worse – by creating a whole new set of problems that you and others must deal with. And that's not all!

Addressing performance problems is also where you and your organization face some huge risks and liabilities if not handled properly. Some of these risks are legal (i.e., lawsuits). Others involve employee morale, productivity, and your organization's reputation. And all of this affects the level of trust that you enjoy – or miss out on – with your people. That's why punishment needs to be seen (and used) as a last resort rather than a primary strategy.

But, You're Only Human

If it hasn't happened yet, sooner or later it will: you'll be faced with an employee who does something disruptive, violates a rule, or just fails to get the job done. He or she has a performance problem. And like it or not, **you** must deal with it.

Of course, it's irritating! You already have plenty on your plate. Now this new problem hits you in the gut like a "Maalox moment" – and it hurts. It's tempting, at first, to want to take that pain and transfer it to the source … to lash out, in a hurtful and punishing way, at the person who caused the problem. While doing so *may* produce some short-term results (not to mention satisfying any initial desires for retribution on your part), such a punitive response typically has long-term negative consequences on working relationships. That makes it a lousy option.

Besides, you really *DO* care about being fair and dealing with people appropriately. You also know that other people will probably hear about any unfair treatment (real or just perceived) on your part. So, now you face another temptation. Out of concern for maintaining relationships at all costs and not being labeled "the heavy," you're tempted to let the issue slide.

Failing to act, however, sends the message that meeting performance standards isn't really that important. Pretty soon, the problem spreads – overlapping into other areas. As the problems mount, so does your misery. Eventually, *your* job is in jeopardy. And that's an even *worse* option!

A Better Way

When facing employee performance problems, leaders often feel caught in "either/or" situations – having to choose between two equally important end states:

Get Results *or* Maintain Relationships.

But you don't have to sacrifice one for the other. Performance results and positive relationships are not mutually exclusive … you *can* achieve both! How? By conducting effective problem-solving discussions with employees – conversations that not only engage people in meeting their job responsibilities, but also pass the test of fair and consistent treatment.

Here's one you can take to the bank: While punishment should be avoided, *discipline doesn't need to be!* Discipline should be about helping employees understand what's expected of them … about solving problems, achieving desired levels of performance, and getting results.

You see, discipline isn't an action that you – the person with authority – must take against employees for misbehavior. Instead, it's a process to help people make good choices about working together safely, ethically, and productively. By focusing on problem solving and treating employees as "adults," you can avoid much of the pain and negativity that typically exists. It's a better and less stressful approach – for your employees and for YOU!

You maintain good discipline when you give employees meaningful responsibilities and then hold them accountable. When people perform well, they deserve credit for their good work. But when they don't perform as expected, you must remind them of their responsibilities and provide them with the opportunity to correct the problem.

Doing those things consistently not only produces desired results, it also builds good working relationships. People know what to expect, and trust is much easier to maintain.

A sports team that plays with discipline is a team that executes well. A person with a disciplined approach to saving for the future is considered wise and mature. These perspectives show us that discipline is more than people just complying with rules and expectations … or else! It's positive because it's based upon commitment — people choosing to do what's right because *they* believe in it and *they* are involved in the process.

Yes, discipline can (and should) be a positive process that produces positive results. And when it comes to addressing performance problems, the way you *get* those results is by applying this time-tested, five-step model (explained, in detail, on the pages that follow):

POSITIVE DISCIPLINE®
PERFORMANCE IMPROVEMENT PROCESS

IDENTIFY *the problem*

ANALYZE *the severity*

DISCUSS *the issue*

DOCUMENT *the discussion*

FOLLOW UP *on the correction*

HOW TO IDENTIFY A PERFORMANCE PROBLEM

At the most basic level, a performance problem is a "gap." It's the difference between what you *expect* versus the employee's *actual* work performance, attendance, or conduct. The wider the gap, the bigger the problem ... and the more intense your headache as a leader.

Obviously, your goal is to close the performance gap. And to do that, you'll need to conduct a calm and straightforward problem-solving discussion – one in which the employee acknowledges that there is a problem and then makes a commitment to fix it. Sound too good to be true? Well, it's not – if you do it right! And the two keys to doing it right are **thinking** and **preparation**.

When facing a performance problem, don't let emotions drive you to a knee-jerk reaction. Everyone loses when that happens. Instead, use your head. Make sure you understand the nature of the performance gap so you'll be able to address it more effectively ... and be able to clearly explain it to the employee when you're ready to talk.

Defining the Problem

The best way to begin the problem-solving process is by preparing *behavioral statements* that identify both DESIRED and ACTUAL performance. Behavioral statements are descriptions of things people *say* and *do*. These statements lay out the facts and establish a clear and specific performance gap. For example:

DESIRED: *Everyone is expected to complete and submit all daily reports before leaving at the end of the day.*

ACTUAL: *On Monday and Wednesday of this week, you left work without turning in your daily reports.*

15

Taking this approach will help you avoid a huge mistake made by many managers: defining and, therefore, communicating performance problems using vague and judgmental terms:

> *"You've caused a lot of screw-ups lately because of your*
> *lazy attitude toward your paperwork!"*

Statements like this tend to be loaded with subjective and judgmental terms that are likely to set off emotional, defensive reactions in people. Remember that words such as "a lot," "screw-ups," "lately," and "lazy attitude" are merely opinions and conclusions. And as such, they open the floodgates of additional problems that can cause painful discussions.

Focus on the Facts

The most important part of defining (and understanding) a performance problem is separating the *facts* from your *judgments and opinions*. Facts are observable – the things you know for sure because they are seen or heard. Judgments, on the other hand, represent opinions and conclusions. They are relative and subjective. They attack the person rather than the problem – increasing the odds that the employee will respond defensively. And that gets in the way of effective problem solving.

But what if my judgment is correct and accurate? you may ask. Well, that really doesn't matter! Opinions are debatable ("I don't do that a lot" … "There's nothing wrong with my attitude"), but it's hard to dispute facts. So don't get hung up with judgments and generalities. If you *have* the facts, stick to them. If you *don't have* the facts, GET THEM … *before* you talk! That way, you and the employee can spend your time working on solutions rather than debating the existence of problems. And that's one **less** headache for you!

PROBLEM STATEMENT EXAMPLES
VAGUE/JUDGMENTAL vs. SPECIFIC/FACTUAL

Your attendance has been totally unacceptable.

vs.

Desired: *You are expected to report to work, each day, as scheduled. However…*

Actual: *You had two unexcused absences last week, and yesterday you were forty-five minutes late.*

You don't respond quickly enough to your messages.

vs.

Desired: *All Service Representatives are expected to respond to customer e-mail messages within twenty-four hours of the time assigned. However…*

Actual: *Computer reports for last week show responses out at twenty-nine hours, thirty-four hours, and thirty-six hours after the time they were assigned to you.*

You're rude to our clients.

vs.

Desired: *Everyone is expected to provide callers with directions to our facility. However…*

Actual: *Yesterday, I heard you tell a caller, "I'm really slammed right now. Why don't you just go to MapQuest and get directions?"*

See the difference?

THE ALL-TOO-COMMON TRAP
TO AVOID

THE POSITIVE DISCIPLINE PATH
TO TAKE

THE ALL-TOO-COMMON TRAP	THE POSITIVE DISCIPLINE PATH
You observe or hear about an employee's specific negative behaviors (facts)	You observe or hear about an employee's specific negative behaviors (facts)
↓	↓
You lump those behaviors (facts) together into a general conclusion and/or judgment about the offender	You use those problematic behaviors (facts) as the problem definition/description
	During the discussion ...
↓	↓
You use that conclusion or judgment as the problem definition/description	You communicate that definition/description to the employee
During the discussion ...	*As a result ...*
↓	↓
You communicate that definition/description to the employee	The employee is more likely to accept the facts and respond COOPERATIVELY
As a result ...	
↓	
The employee is more likely to reject your description and respond DEFENSIVELY	

ANALYZING THE SEVERITY OF THE PROBLEM

Working with employees to resolve performance problems is one of your key leadership responsibilities. How well you meet that responsibility will depend on your ability to fully understand the nature of each problem you face. By identifying DESIRED and ACTUAL performance, you began building that understanding. But, there's more you need to know, and more you need to do, *before* meeting with the employee.

Since no two people are exactly the same, the problems they exhibit will come in a variety of "shapes and sizes." As a result, there is no automatic, one-size-fits-all response to employee deficiencies. You must select the response that is appropriate for each circumstance. That's where **analyzing problem severity** comes in.

Once you're sure that a gap between desired and actual performance clearly exists, you'll need to assess just how severe that gap is. Doing that involves answering questions such as:

◆ **Why is it important that this problem be resolved?**

◆ **What should/will happen to the employee if the problem continues?**

◆ **What kind of discussion should be conducted?**

Obviously, the greater the problem severity, the higher the stakes involved ... and the more serious and expeditious your response needs to be. But regardless of the circumstances, the response you select needs to be constructive, respectful, and – whenever possible – *positive* in nature.

A Better Set of "Why's"

Even when faced with the facts of a performance gap, an employee may not fully understand (or buy into) the importance of resolving the problem; the "why" of taking corrective action may not be clear or apparent. The traditional management response to this is justifying "why" from a position of power and authority – making statements like, *Because I'm the boss! … Because it's a rule!* (watch the person's eyes glaze over on that one!) … *Because I said so!* But a power and authority approach rarely helps you engage a person in cooperative problem solving. Instead, it tends to result in the employee becoming defensive and resentful. Not good … for either of you!

Analyzing problem severity *before* your discussion, and then using that information to obtain the employee's agreement to correct the problem, is a much more effective approach. You're able to provide the employee with valid reasons for making a commitment to change – reasons that are easier to accept than "my boss told me to." And, you're in a better position to determine what kind of discussion you need to conduct (coaching, counseling, or formal discipline).

So, how do you analyze the level of problem severity? You do it by examining and considering two factors: IMPACT and CONSEQUENCES.

Determining the IMPACT

Simply put, IMPACT is the various ways the performance problem negatively affects your operation, your customers, other members of your team … and YOU, as the leader. Determining the IMPACT gives you a better understanding of the problem. And, it arms you with the good (valid) business reasons why the problem must be solved – reasons you'll communicate to the employee during the discussion.

Using the example problem of failing to turn in daily reports, an IMPACT list might include things like:

1. Overall department reports will be incomplete and inaccurate.

2. Management may make bad decisions based on incomplete data.

3. It causes scheduling problems and creates more work for others.

4. Customer orders or services may be delayed.

5. Additional management time and paperwork is required to correct resulting problems.

IMPACT establishes your right and obligation to require a change. It also provides the employee with practical reasons *why* he or she should cooperate and agree to solve the problem – minimizing the chances that your expectations will be perceived as being arbitrary or unfair. Even if the employee doesn't like hearing the reasons you provide, at least he or she will know that your requirements are based upon business-related facts. That makes it more likely that he or she will accept responsibility for the problem and that positive action will take place.

Determining the CONSEQUENCES

Occasionally, you may encounter an employee who will not agree with your assessment of the problem – even after hearing how he or she is negatively impacting others. A few (*very* few) people just won't "get it" unless they see how it affects **them** personally. That's why, *before* meeting with the employee, you'll also want to determine the CONSEQUENCES.

CONSEQUENCES are the negative outcomes the employee may/will experience if the problem isn't satisfactorily resolved. Don't mistake these as "threats" – that's not what they're about. Consequences are logical, predictable outcomes resulting from an employee's failure to live up to his or her responsibilities.

A typical CONSEQUENCES list includes things like:

1. Damage to your [the employee's] professional reputation.

2. Damage to your relationships with fellow team members.

3. Limited or no merit increases.

4. Reduced opportunities for development and advancement.

5. Closer supervision.

6. Reassignment and/or demotion.

7. More serious formal disciplinary action – up to and including termination of employment.

For consequences to be valid and effective, they must be: a) outcomes that the employee will likely perceive as being undesirable, and b) actions that you really *will* take (or recommend) if the problem isn't fixed.

The history and severity of the problem – along with the level of cooperation displayed by the employee – will dictate how you'll communicate and use IMPACT and CONSEQUENCES during the discussion (more about this in the next chapter). Your analysis assures that you'll be ready and confident to discuss *both* whenever appropriate.

Deciding What Type of Discussion is Appropriate

By "doing your homework" (i.e., thinking, analyzing, investigating, and preparing), you'll surface key facts to help determine what type of a discussion you should conduct.

Most of the time, problem solving will not involve any type of formal discipline. Instead, you'll have an informal conversation to "nip the problem in the bud" by reminding the employee of your expectations and his or her responsibilities.

However, if you're dealing with a continuing problem, a major rule infraction, or an issue with established precedence ("past practice") that you're expected to follow, a more serious approach may be in order.

And, on rare occasions, a performance problem may be so severe (theft, assault, etc.) that termination is appropriate – even if no previous disciplinary action has taken place.

Because of the obvious legal risks involved, be sure to check with the proper organizational authorities before taking any type of formal disciplinary action – and be sure to follow your organizational procedures to the letter.

Time to Talk

Once you've identified the performance gap, evaluated and listed the IMPACT and CONSEQUENCES of the problem, and determined what type of discussion is appropriate, it's time to talk with the employee.

The discussion is the primary problem-solving activity … it's what you've prepared for up to this point … it's "where the rubber meets the road."

PERFORMANCE PROBLEM DISCUSSION
PREPARATION CHECKLIST

☐ Identify the DESIRED and ACTUAL performance in specific, behavioral terms. *Write them down.*

☐ Determine the negative IMPACT of the problem – the ways others are affected – in specific terms. *Write them down.*

☐ Identify the realistic CONSEQUENCES the employee will face if the problem is not resolved. *Write them down.*

☐ Check "past practices." Have similar problems occurred elsewhere in the organization? How were they handled?

☐ Determine what type of discussion is appropriate: Coaching? Counseling? Formal Discipline?

☐ Seek counsel and obtain necessary approvals if formal discipline is involved.

| DISCUSS |

CONDUCTING THE PROBLEM-SOLVING DISCUSSION

Without question, the most critical component of the problem-solving process is the **discussion**. How you handle this activity will, with few exceptions, shape the employee's response, the outcome, and the nature of your long-term relationship with each other.

The Goal

As mentioned earlier, the goal of the discussion is to **gain the employee's agreement** to make a positive change. This is important for two reasons:

1. **If the person agrees to solve the problem, he or she is more likely to actually correct it.**

2. **If the person does not correct the problem (after talking with you), the next discussion will focus not only on the continuing problem, but also on his or her failure to live up to the prior commitment – making it a far more serious situation.**

By gaining agreement, you put the responsibility for a performance problem right where it belongs: squarely on the shoulders of the person who *owns* it. And if that problem isn't corrected, it's very powerful to be able to point out, *You didn't do what you said you would do.* Instead of you being "the heavy," it becomes clear that the employee is in the wrong … *he or she* is the one who's being unfair.

The Discussion Stages

Okay, now you're prepared. You and the employee are in a location with appropriate privacy and it's time to talk. If you address the problem in a structured, businesslike way, you're much more likely to gain a real commitment from the employee. Do this right, and there's an excellent chance the problem will go away for good … and you'll have one *less* headache.

So, how *does* one "do it right"? You do it by working your way through the following stages of a POSITIVE DISCIPLINE problem-solving discussion:

STAGE I – Start With a Non-Accusatory Opening

The first few seconds of the conversation are critical to your ultimate success. Avoid beginning with "you statements" like, *You have a problem.* While those words may be true, they also tend to make people more anxious and defensive. Instead, use a non-accusatory opening that asks for the employee's cooperation: ***I need your help to solve a problem.***

Eliminate any long-winded speeches intended either to prove you are "in the right" or to sugarcoat the issues. Get right to the point by immediately moving to the next stage.

STAGE II – Describe DESIRED and ACTUAL Performance

It doesn't matter which you begin with – but it is important that you explain *both* so the employee can clearly understand the performance gap.

Present your DESIRED and ACTUAL performance descriptions (developed before the discussion) *verbatim*. Doing so will help you avoid the common traps of lecturing, forgetting important facts, and inserting vague or judgmental words – traps that lead to arguments instead of agreements. Be calm, brief, and to the point – just like you'd want it if *you* were in the "hot seat."

STAGE III – Seek an Explanation

Once you've described the problem, you'll want to find out what the employee has to say about it. Ask an open-ended question such as, *What happened?* or *What's going on?* This gets the employee involved in the discussion. And it gives you the opportunity to demonstrate respect by listening to, and talking about, what he or she has to say.

In all likelihood, the employee will offer an explanation as to why a problem exists or why something went wrong. You'll want to listen carefully, and probe as necessary, to make sure you fully understand what he or she is saying.

What are you listening *for*? Obstacles or circumstances that the employee could not control! Examples of these include: equipment malfunctions, training discrepancies, conflicting instructions from a higher authority (or from YOU), and lack of cooperation from another department. Should you hear such explanations, you'll want to suspend the discussion so you can investigate the matter further. Schedule a time to reconvene. When you meet again, present your findings and work with the person to develop a strategy for handling similar occurrences in the future.

Most of the time, however, it will be clear that the problem resulted from factors *within* the employee's control. He or she *could* have met performance requirements like everyone else, but didn't. And it's not unusual that you'll hear one or more excuses that the person believes (or at least *hopes*) are reasonable and valid. Your reaction to these will affect whether the employee becomes defensive or moves toward understanding and responsibility.

Of course there are reasons why things go wrong – but don't get hung up on critiquing excuses or debating over who is to *blame*. You're wise if you avoid assuming a "judge of excuses" role. Think about it. If you respond with something like *That's not a good reason!* (or worse yet, *That's a lame excuse!*), the person may argue, clam up and withdraw, or just continue offering new excuses for the same problem. With any of these scenarios, you can easily lose control of the discussion and end up *without* the employee's commitment to change.

Once you're sure that the employee is responsible for the problem – and that he or she has the ability to solve it – calmly and deliberately MOVE ON!

STAGE IV – Ask for Agreement

By this point, you've explained DESIRED and ACTUAL performance, involved the employee in the discussion, developed an understanding of any reasons provided, and taken care to demonstrate respect with good listening. Now, return the conversation to the performance gap. Ask the employee for his or her agreement: *Do you see why this is important? Can I count on you to solve this problem?*

Usually, an employee who is dealt with in a respectful manner will agree to solve a problem after you bring the facts to his or her attention. Once that happens, go directly to the next discussion stage: Discuss Possible Solutions. However, if the employee fails to agree, you should immediately review the IMPACT list. Explain these good business reasons for solving the problem and ask for the employee's agreement.

Sometimes, you may encounter an employee who – even after hearing how the problem is impacting others – is hesitant to give his or her agreement. If that's the case, your next move is to clearly describe the specific CONSEQUENCES – the logical outcomes the employee can expect if the problem isn't resolved. Present your list in a clear and straightforward manner. Then, once again, ask the employee for his or her agreement to solve the problem. You'll likely get some kind of an agreement after the CONSEQUENCES are discussed – allowing you to proceed to the next stage. Don't comment on the begrudging nature of the response. Once again, just MOVE ON!

On rare occasions – even after hearing the consequences at hand – an employee may still refuse to agree. That's a clear demonstration that he or she has no intention of committing to the necessary change. Sure, you would prefer that the person willingly accept his or her responsibility to solve the problem … you'd much rather be dealing in the commitment arena. But if he or she *won't* agree, you still have to get the job done and maintain your performance standards. So, this becomes the time when, as a last resort, you must **mandate compliance**.

To mandate compliance:

A. Review the performance expectation.

B. Explain to the employee that he or she must solve the problem and comply with the rules and standards.

C. Describe any formal corrective action you will be taking at this time (if applicable).

D. Notify the employee that further occurrences may lead to serious disciplinary action – up to and including termination.

E. Confirm that the employee understands your mandate.

F. Close by expressing your confidence that the employee can correct this problem if he or she chooses to do so.

Note: If it becomes necessary to mandate compliance, you will not proceed to the next stage. The discussion will conclude with your mandate.

Question: **If it becomes necessary to mandate compliance, has the process failed** … will my efforts have been wasted?

Answer: **Not at all!** You've still demonstrated good leadership. You've proven that you treat people respectfully – giving them chances to respond to their deficiencies in an adult, businesslike manner. And, you've reinforced the fact that employees are responsible and accountable for their own performance. You can be confident that you are doing the right thing for the right reasons – even when it's not easy!

Fortunately, you won't need to mandate compliance that often. In most cases, merely asking for agreement will produce a positive employee response and allow you to move to the next stage.

STAGE V – Discuss Possible Solutions

You probably have good ideas about what works and how to accomplish expectations. Keep in mind, however, that it's the *employee's* responsibility to resolve the problem, not yours.

The last thing in the world you should do after gaining the employee's agreement is say something like, *Great, now here's what I want you to do ….* Your job is to facilitate the discussion so that the person understands the problem and is given an opportunity to correct it. Be prepared to offer suggestions if asked, but give the employee a chance to come up with his or her own solutions. Why do it that way? The answer is simple: **Ownership!**

People tend to work harder for their own ideas. Solutions they participate in developing become commitments that are much more likely to yield quick and permanent results.

You can guide the employee in identifying (and committing to) solutions by asking three simple questions:

1. **What specifically can you do … by when?**
   (This helps the person pinpoint specific actions.)

2. **Can you think of anything that would prevent you from doing that?**
   (This helps identify potential obstacles and eliminates future excuses.)

3. **Will you do that?**
   (This locks in the employee's agreement/commitment.)

People often respond to the first question with *I'll do my best* or *I'll try harder.* These aren't solutions – they're just statements … with lots of "wiggle room." If you hear them, respond by telling the employee that you appreciate his or her cooperation, and then ask, "What specifically will you do to carry out these good intentions?" You need a measurable action – otherwise the chances are slim that you'll actually see a change.

A few words of caution:

◆ Don't accept solutions that are complicated and unrealistic – or ones that you truly believe fall short of correcting the problem. Keep challenging the employee to come up with something that will work.

◆ Offer suggestions if the person is struggling for ideas, but don't get frustrated or become defensive if he or she rejects your solutions. Keep an open mind. Just because you would do things differently doesn't mean that an employee's idea won't work.

◆ Occasionally, an employee may ask *you* to help fix the problem. If you receive such a request, determine if your participation is appropriate. Just remember that if you agree to do something, the employee needs to do something as well. If there's no commitment on the employee's part, *you'll* end up owning the solution instead of him or her.

As you conclude this stage of the discussion, you should confirm the employee's commitment. Summarize the actions that have been agreed to – along with any timelines for accomplishment.

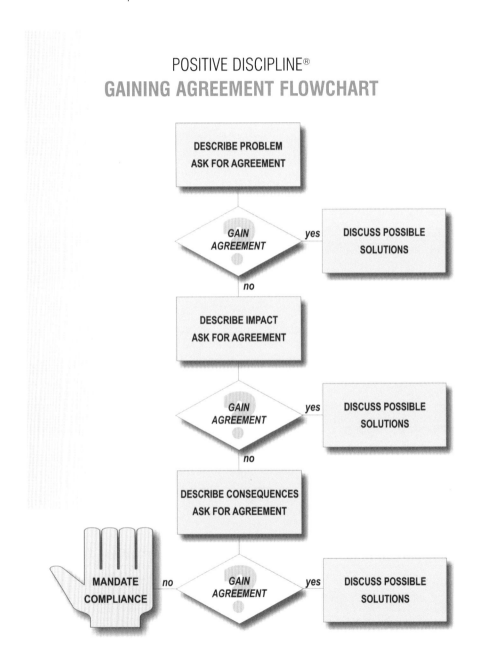

POSITIVE DISCIPLINE®
GAINING AGREEMENT FLOWCHART

STAGE VI – If Formal Discipline Is Involved, Provide Notification
Note: Skip this stage if not applicable.

Even if the employee cooperated in the discussion, the problem may be so severe that a level of formal disciplinary action is warranted. Follow your organization's procedures in describing what level of formal disciplinary action you're taking – along with all related administrative details.

STAGE VII – End on a Positive Note

One of the best ways to close the discussion is to express your confidence in the employee's ability to solve the problem. Communicate your belief (and expectation) that the agreed upon action(s) will produce the desired results. Thank the person for his or her cooperation. And reinforce how correcting the problem contributes to everyone's success.

Your positive expectations will help preserve the employee's self-esteem and encourage follow-through on his or her commitment.

CONDUCTING THE DISCUSSION
CHECKLIST

☐ Use a non-accusatory opening ("I need your help to solve a problem.").

☐ Identify the performance gap by describing DESIRED and ACTUAL performance.

☐ Request an explanation. Ask open-ended questions. Listen to, and discuss, what the employee has to say.

☐ Ask for the employee's agreement to solve the problem. If necessary, discuss IMPACT, discuss CONSEQUENCES, and mandate compliance.

☐ Discuss alternative solutions. Summarize the action plan(s) and confirm the employee's commitment.

☐ Explain if formal disciplinary action applies.

☐ Close on a positive note.

DOCUMENT | DOCUMENTING THE PROBLEM ... AND THE DISCUSSION

The *What's* & *Why's* of Documentation

Do you associate documentation with legal requirements ... with supporting your "case" against an employee ... with protecting you and your organization from claims of unfair treatment? Well, as important as those are, they're not the only reasons for making written records. Documentation should also support your problem-solving efforts. It's a tool for ensuring that everyone is informed and stays on the right track. Therefore, truly effective documentation not only records what the *employee* did (the problem), but also what YOU did (*your* problem-solving efforts).

Certainly, if you are conducting a formal conversation, you should document the discussion and distribute copies according to your company's administrative procedures for disciplinary actions. However, even with informal discussions, it's a good idea to keep some kind of record for future reference purposes. So, you'll want to make notes as you talk.

Sometimes, as you're taking notes, an employee may exhibit concern about what you're doing and why you're doing it. If that occurs, explain that you're jotting down a few key points to help you remember what was discussed and prevent any misunderstandings that might come up later. Show the employee what you've written so he or she knows that you've recorded nothing but facts. And describe what you'll be doing with the information after the discussion. Doing that can remove the mystery from documentation ... and a lot of the fear of being unfairly "written up."

The Key Points of Documentation

For serious (or continuing) performance problems, you'll want to convert your notes into a more structured written record – one that describes the PROBLEM, the HISTORY, and the DISCUSSION. Consider doing this in a memo format – addressed to the employee rather than merely "to file." And, be sure to give him or her a copy. That way, there are no secrets … no hidden agendas … no mistrust.

When describing the PROBLEM

✓ Use facts and specifics, not generalities or judgments.

✓ Include descriptions of DESIRED and ACTUAL performance.

✓ Include the IMPACT and CONSEQUENCES you identified.

When describing the HISTORY

✓ State how long the problem has existed.

✓ Mention any previous discussions about the problem and any prior formal disciplinary action that may have been taken.

✓ Indicate if the employee has failed to live up to any agreements made in prior discussions.

When describing the DISCUSSION

✓ Indicate the date, time, and location of the conversation.

✓ Include specific comments and statements made by the employee – including his or her agreement.

✓ List all actions the employee said he or she would take to correct the problem.

✓ In those rare instances where you were unable to gain an agreement, include what you told the employee when mandating compliance.

Keep It Factual and Future Oriented

Documentation shouldn't be merely an administrative requirement in order to pass reviews by management or a litigation-related "third party" down the road. It should also be a tool that supports and furthers your performance improvement activities.

It can serve *both* of those purposes if you stick to the facts and focus on your efforts to produce a positive behavior change in the future – rather than emphasizing blame and penalties for past misbehavior.

Remember that your purpose is *not* to "write THEM up" – it's to write IT down. There is a difference!

DOCUMENTATION EXAMPLE

TO: M. Ployee
FROM: D. Manager
DATE: June 11, 20__
SUBJECT: WORK PERFORMANCE DISCUSSION

This memo summarizes our discussion, today, at 9:00 a.m. in the conference room regarding a work performance issue. Each team member is expected to complete and submit all daily reports before leaving at the end of the day. However, on both Monday and Wednesday of this week, you left work without turning in your reports. We talked about this issue before on May 4 – at which time you agreed that you would submit your reports as expected.

Today, you said that you didn't see why this was "such a big deal." I responded by explaining the impact of the problem ... that when all daily reports are not completed and submitted on time:

1. Department statistics will be incomplete and inaccurate;
2. Management may make bad decisions based on incomplete data;
3. It causes scheduling problems and creates more work for others;
4. Customer orders or services may be delayed;
5. Additional management time and paperwork is required to correct resulting problems.

You then said that you have many other priorities you feel are more important than the daily reports. Although you do have other important responsibilities, I re-emphasized that the reports must be completed because of their importance to our overall operation. I also informed you of the potential negative consequences you could expect if the problem continues – up to and including formal disciplinary action.

You told me that you now understand the importance of this expectation and you agreed to have all reports completed and turned in as required. You said that you will set aside a time period in the last 30 minutes of each workday to complete and submit your reports, and that you will contact me for clarification of priorities if you have a conflict.

I believe that putting your solution into practice will resolve this issue. Thank you for your commitment to keep on track with our department's standards.

FOLLOWING WITH "FOLLOW-UP"

Okay. You survived a few sleepless nights, you did your "homework" (thinking and preparation), you had the discussion, and the employee cooperated – he or she agreed to solve the problem. Whew! So, cross *that* one off the list ... case closed ... you're done ... time to move on to other things. Right? Not quite! The POSITIVE DISCIPLINE process isn't complete until you FOLLOW UP.

Admittedly, it's easy to overlook the importance of following up on problem-solving discussions – especially when you're busy. But, fail to get back together and the employee may be left with some very negative perceptions, such as:

◆ *I haven't heard a word since we talked. My "problem" must not have been all that serious to begin with;*

◆ *Obviously, my boss focuses on the past, not the future;*

◆ *You get zero credit for correcting problems around here;*

◆ *I just have to say what the boss wants to hear during the discussion and then I can forget about it.*

There's no way you want these poor impressions to get in the way of your results and relationships. So review the action plans the employee identified, determine whether or not the problem has been corrected, and get together for a follow-up session.

If the problem HAS been solved ...

... meet with the employee to recognize the good performance and thank him or her for living up to the commitment. Such positive reinforcement helps to keep people on the right track. And it pays dividends into the future! The next time you need to talk about performance improvement, you have a good experience to build upon.

Let's face it, many people get nervous seeing the boss coming – and it's no wonder if all they ever hear from you is *bad news*. But you can reduce or eliminate these jitters if you also show up *when things get better*. Positive follow-up builds stronger trust in you and your problem-solving process; it demonstrates that working together to solve problems really IS in both of your best interests.

If the problem HASN'T been corrected ...

... you'll need to find out why, and then take the appropriate action. Perhaps the corrective action(s) agreed upon didn't work as expected. You and the employee should review this and come up with an alternative plan. If the problem severity is not great and there are conditions that indicate the employee needs help fine-tuning the solution(s), your strategy may be to conduct another coaching or counseling discussion.

If, however, the employee merely failed to deliver on his or her agreement (or, in rare cases, comply with a mandate) you'll need to ratchet up the accountability with a more serious conversation – even one in which you take formal disciplinary action (according to your organization's administrative procedures). Your follow-up provides factual justification for taking such action when an employee can't, or won't, make the necessary improvements.

Follow-Up Timing

Did you set a specific date or time frame for problem correction? If so, you'd better make sure that's when you follow up. But there are also situations that may require you to observe a pattern of performance before you can discuss it again. In those cases, make a note to look for events or patterns that will trigger your follow-up.

Remember that employees will determine what's truly important by watching what you pay ongoing attention to. Following up is how you prove that problem solving is for real; it's how you demonstrate that everyone must make good choices, get desired results, and do what they say they will do.

Whether people solve problems or they don't, a response from you is warranted. And you won't know what type of response is appropriate unless you look, listen, investigate, and *follow up!*

A SUMMARY REVIEW

POSITIVE DISCIPLINE®
PERFORMANCE IMPROVEMENT PROCESS

IDENTIFY — ... the problem using specific descriptions of **desired performance** vs. **actual performance**

ANALYZE — ... the severity of the problem by examining its **impact**, the **consequences** the employee will face if not corrected, and **"past practices"** for similar situations

DISCUSS — ... the problem. Gain the employee's **agreement** and identify **action plans**. Inform the employee if formal discipline is involved

DOCUMENT — ... the nature of the **problem**, the **history** of the problem, and what was said in the **discussion**

FOLLOW UP — ... to **recognize improvement** or **take appropriate action** if the problem has not been corrected

TIPS FOR ENCOURAGING GOOD PERFORMANCE

Throughout this book, we've shown you how to confront problems in a manner that's positive and more effective than traditional, punitive approaches. But as important as that is, it's only *part* of what you must do to manage overall employee performance – particularly if you're looking to enjoy superior results on a regular basis. To get those results, the best leaders know that it's critical to be **PROactive** ... to work at *preventing* problems from occurring in the first place!

Here's another one you can take to the bank: The more *proactive* you are, the less *reactive* you'll need to be! Encouraging superior performance minimizes the number of performance problems you'll have to deal with – and the number of management headaches that come with them. Your workforce will be more committed to organizational goals. You'll have more time for other priorities. And, you'll enhance the trust and working relationships you enjoy with team members – a big part of what makes POSITIVE DISCIPLINE so *positive.*

Proactive Performance Management Strategies

Notice Patterns of Performance

Watch for patterns suggesting an employee may be heading for trouble. If you see any early indicators, put on your **coaching** hat. Help the person recognize the performance pitfalls *before* sliding down the "slippery slope."

Attendance issues are a good example. It may take weeks or months before tardiness or absences become so problematic that they require disciplinary action. Be proactive – don't wait. As soon as you start to see a change in an attendance pattern, talk to the person. Remind him or her of the importance of being at work … and being there on time. This shows that it matters when he or she isn't there. It also provides an opportunity for you to uncover underlying problems that may be causing these changes so you can deal with them early in the cycle.

Work performance patterns typically require more time to identify and may take longer to correct. As soon as you see performance start to turn in the wrong direction, provide coaching to help the person deal with any difficulties. And remember that it may take a while for the person to get back to standard.

Employee **conduct** is different. Conduct requiring disciplinary measures is more immediate and typically based upon specific behavior lapses. Even so, there often are warning signs: smaller infractions that are problematic, but not severe violations. We sometimes see these as indicating "a change in attitude." [Just remember that your judgment about someone's attitude is based on observed *behaviors*.] It's much easier to deal with those behaviors if you start coaching early – before serious infractions occur.

Provide Training

One of the very best proactive performance management strategies is making sure that each employee has the knowledge and skills to meet job expectations. Ask yourself this question: *How sure am I that the employee has received proper training in all aspects of the job?* Unless you're absolutely convinced that the training received has been adequate and appropriate, arrange for more.

You probably have a variety of developmental resources at your disposal – such as manuals, classes, computer-based programs, and on-the-job training. So use them! Training is a sound investment that can pay huge dividends.

Remove Obstacles

This strategy proves you're serious about promoting success – and it reduces frustration caused by things that are beyond the employee's control. To uncover obstacles, ask yourself: *Is there anything that prevents the employee from choosing to do the job right?*

Obstacles can be overt and easy to uncover (e.g., a lack of time, tools, and necessary resources), or they can be subtle and harder to detect (unclear instructions; conflicting messages or priorities; etc.). Not sure if an employee is facing a performance obstacle? ASK!

Once you've determined that an obstacle exists, take action to eliminate it. If you don't have the authority or ability to make the necessary change(s), go to someone who does and solicit his or her help. Some obstacles – things like limited budgets, outside regulations, and organizational procedures – *can't* be eliminated. Make sure you understand what, if any, latitude you have for dealing with these. Explain to the employee why the hindrance can't be removed. Then, help him or her to come up with plans to get the job done in the best way possible.

Strategies to Keep Discipline In Sync With Values

To build a superior workforce, it's important for employees to know that you and your organization will deal with occasional problem performance in ways that match your values about how people should be treated.

Provide "Reminders"

When addressing performance issues, avoid using the word "warning." That term has negative connotations – it's associated with punishment and often causes resentment that gets in the way of building superior performance. Instead, use the term "reminder."

A reminder not only demonstrates your willingness to hold a person accountable, it also implies that you respect the employee as an adult – one who, with good information and constructive feedback, will choose to live up to his or her responsibilities.

Consider a "Decision Making Leave" (DML)

A disciplinary suspension is sometimes used as a way of letting an employee know that his or her job is in jeopardy. But most suspensions, by their very nature, are also punishing – they are about threats and losing one or more day's pay rather than about problem solving and making good choices. A DML is different, and many organizations have found it to be a more effective, values-driven way to deal with serious disciplinary cases.

Typically, a DML involves giving the employee a paid assignment: "Take the next workday off and make a **final decision** to either correct the problem and meet ALL standards of the organization, or to resign."

When issuing a Decision Making Leave, inform the employee you hope he or she chooses to keep working – but that any further problems requiring formal action (during a specified period of time) will likely result in termination of employment.

Experience has shown that employees take DML's very seriously. Most will choose to keep their jobs and make the changes necessary to meet performance expectations. Those who fail have no legitimate excuses. You will have provided every opportunity for them to correct their problems and be successful.

Ultimately, a DML demonstrates that *the employee* must take responsibility for determining his or her own future. It's in sync with positive values about how to treat people *and* it holds people accountable for their performance and behavior.

Strategies for Reinforcing Good Performance

Without a doubt, providing **recognition** is one of the best ways (if not THE best way) to build and maintain superior performance. The reason for that is quite simple: reinforced behavior gets *repeated*. As human beings, we all tend to replicate those actions that bring us pleasure and positive acknowledgement. So, one of your key performance management strategies needs to be *doing right by those who do right!*

Recognition is most effective when it is:

Timely – given as soon as possible after the positive behavior takes place;

Specific – identifies *exactly* what the person did that was so positive;

Personal – delivered in a way that's meaningful for the receiver;

Proportional – is appropriate for the level of positive performance and/or the results achieved.

Recognize Outstanding Performers

These employees have *earned* your attention by taking the initiative to deliver superior performance in one or more areas. Don't overlook them! Although they may not say so, they want credit for what they do. They deserve it!

Provide the recognition and rewards that are commensurate (proportional) with these employees' achievements. Acknowledge (and thank them for) their superior performance as soon as you become aware of it. And make sure they understand the positive impact they are making. Remember that the way you treat these people will determine whether others decide to join their exclusive group in the future.

Recognize Consistently Good Performers

Are you missing opportunities to positively interact with the mainstream employees who are the backbone your organization's success? These are the people who, day in, day out, meet expectations without doing the outstanding things that attract attention. As a result, they are often overlooked and taken for granted.

Sure, it's easy to ignore these folks. After all, they're "just doing their jobs." But think about what would happen if they *didn't*. Would you be able to get the results you want and need? Would the superior members of your team be able to do outstanding things without the support of the "backbone"? Probably not! Therefore, it's critical to appreciate and recognize those who maintain good, solid performance over time.

While it may not be appropriate to provide large rewards for this level of performance, it certainly is right to conduct positive recognition discussions. Pay attention to these people. Support them. Coach them. Appreciate them. Be accessible when they need you. And remember that it's often the small things you do that make a big difference in building people up to become even better performers.

"Outstanding leaders go out of their way
to boost the self-esteem of their personnel.
If people believe in themselves,
it's amazing what they can accomplish."

~ Sam Walton

Recognize Performance Improvement

Now that you know how to effectively deal with problem performers, it's reasonable to assume that most of those folks will be making improvements. You'll want to give them credit for that when you follow up on your discussions; you'll want to reinforce the improved performance so that it will be *repeated*.

Sometimes, leaders assume that employees with performance deficiencies in one area should not be recognized when they do other things well. That's a big mistake! Even people with problems are doing some things right. And each time they do provides you an opportunity to build their confidence and self-esteem … to reinforce what they've done well.

You see, bad work does NOT cancel out good work. They are separate actions that should be dealt with separately and appropriately. Do that, and you'll prove that you care about *total* performance … about helping ALL employees become the best they can be.

Leadership
is the art of getting
someone else to do
what you want done
because he [or she]
wants to do it.

~ Dwight D. Eisenhower

CLOSING THOUGHTS

As a leader, you are a major influence on the performance and behavior of employees – perhaps much more than you realize. When you show a genuine concern for both the work to be done *and* the people who do that work, you have a better chance of achieving positive results and building trust-based relationships. Nowhere is that opportunity greater than in that arena we call "discipline."

It's no secret that discipline can be used as a hammer to pound people down for occasional mistakes or poor results ... as something you DO TO people for misbehavior. But by taking that approach, you run the risk of producing a workforce that is compliance driven – one in need of constant supervision and dependent on the boss (YOU) to solve all the problems. By any measure, that makes your job much harder and less rewarding.

Yes, discipline is necessary. But it doesn't have to be a "necessary evil"! Instead, it should be something you *create and maintain* – because everyone deserves to work in an organization that is safe, productive, and professional.

Fact is, you have a choice on how to use your influence. You can lead in a way that encourages people to check their brains (and their commitment) at the door of your business, or one that promotes responsibility by helping people learn to solve their own problems – quickly and permanently.

The choice is yours. Choose wisely ...
choose POSITIVE DISCIPLINE!

THE AUTHORS

Eric Harvey is a renowned author, consultant, speaker, educator, and president of The WALK THE TALK Company. His thirty-plus years of professional experience are reflected in over thirty highly acclaimed books, including the best-selling *WALK THE TALK ... And Get The Results You Want*, *The Leadership Secrets of Santa Claus®*, *Ethics4Everyone*, and *Leadership Courage*.

Paul Sims, with over thirty years of business experience, has built a solid reputation of getting positive results for client organizations in the areas of leadership, management, and non-punitive discipline. He is co-author of *Nuts'nBolts Leadership* and *Leading to Ethics*.

THE PUBLISHER

For over 30 years, WalkTheTalk.com has been dedicated to one simple goal... one single mission: To provide you and your organization with high-impact resources for your personal and professional success.

Walk The Talk resources are designed to:
- Develop your skills and confidence
- Inspire your team
- Create customer enthusiasm
- Build leadership skills
- Stretch your mind
- Handle tough "people problems"
- Develop a culture of respect and responsibility
- And, most importantly, help you achieve your personal and professional goals.

Contact the Walk The Talk team at
1.888.822.9255
or visit us at www.walkthetalk.com

Other Recommended Resources from WalkTheTalk.com

The Manager's Coaching Handbook – Equip all of your managers, supervisors, and team leaders with simple, easy-to-follow guidelines for positively affecting employee performance. Within these pages you'll find practical strategies for dealing with superior performers, those with performance problems, and everyone in between!

Only **$10.95** (Quantity discounts available.)

The Walk the Talk Top 10 Bestsellers Library

Contains 10 of our best-selling "how to" books in one convenient package. From basic leadership strategies and concepts – to ethics, coaching, and motivation techniques – your leaders will be equipped to take everyone in your organization to higher levels of performance and productivity. Only **$85.00**

To learn more about our hundreds of resources designed to help managers become more effective and respected leaders, visit www.WalkTheTalk.com

Resources for Personal and Professional Success